Emergency Funds 101

Surviving and Thriving in a Crisis

Table of Contents

Chapter 1. Introduction

In this Special Report, "Emergency Funds 101: Surviving and Thriving in a Crisis," we break down the nitty-gritty of emergency financial planning in an accessible, easy-to-understand format. No complex financial jargon, just clear, simple instructions and advice designed to cushion you through life's unforeseen storms. Explore how to start, build, and effectively utilize an emergency fund, all the while developing a financial resilience that not only helps you 'weather the storm', but also prosper amidst adversity. This engaging, real-world approach to personal finance is more than a guide; it's your gateway to a more secure and worry-free future. Bursting with practical tips, case studies, and expert insights, this report is an investment unto itself - ensuring you're not just merely surviving in a crisis, but truly thriving!

Chapter 2. Understanding Emergency Funds: The Basics

In emergencies, we often scramble to piece together a financial solution, causing stress and uncertainty. An emergency fund serves as a financial safety net, allowing you to cover unexpected costs without relying on credit or loans. Let's delve into the details, so you understand the basics, the importance, and the right approach to building an emergency fund.

2.1. Understanding What An Emergency Fund Is

Simply put, an emergency fund is a stash of money set aside to cover the financial surprises life throws your way. These unexpected expenses can range from a job loss, significant health expenses, an urgent home or auto repair, legal issues, or any cost that is unplanned and urgent. An emergency fund is precisely that - money that is saved for emergencies, not future expenses that are predictable like your child's college fees or your annual vacation.

2.2. The Purpose of An Emergency Fund: Why is it Important?

An emergency fund plays a compelling role in maintaining financial stability and safeguarding mental and emotional wellbeing. Here are a few reasons why:

1. **Financial Stability**: Emergencies are unpredictable. In the event of sudden unemployment or significant medical costs, having money in reserve can mean the difference between staying afloat and going into debt.

2. **Mental Peace**: Money-related stress is fertile ground for anxiety. An emergency fund can offer peace of mind knowing you have a financial buffer.

3. **Avoidance of Debt**: Absence of an emergency fund may push you towards high-interest credit card debt or loans.

4. **Guard Against Credit Dependence**: Having an emergency fund helps you stay independent and not resort to credit for unexpected expenses.

2.3. Size Matters: How Much Should Your Emergency Fund Be?

Before starting to build an emergency fund, it's crucial to determine how much you need to save. Financial advisors suggest that your emergency fund should cover three to six months of your living expenses, but the final figure will differ for everyone. This hefty sum may seem daunting but remember, you don't have to save it all at once.

Calculate your monthly expenses, including everything from mortgage or rent, groceries, utility bills, insurance premiums, to personal expenses. Then, multiply this figure by the number of months you aim to cover. This multiplication should give you an ideal amount for your emergency fund.

2.4. Building Your Emergency Fund: A Step-by-Step Guide

Once you know how much you need to save, you can start the process of building your emergency fund. Here's a step-by-step guide:

1. **Establish a Monthly Budget**: Assess your income and expenses and determine a feasible savings target every month. Stick to this

budget to ensure you're consistently setting money aside.

2. **Start Small**: Don't be demotivated if you can only afford to set aside a small amount each month. Remember, even the tallest mountain can be climbed, one step at a time.

3. **Choose the Right Account**: Your emergency fund should be easily accessible. Consider using a high-yield savings account, which offers a higher interest rate than a regular savings account.

4. **Build Saving Habits**: Make saving automatic. Set up automatic transfers to your savings account right after you receive your paycheck.

5. **Extra Money Goes into Fund**: Any extra money, such as tax refunds or bonuses, should go into your emergency fund.

2.5. Using Your Emergency Fund: A Matter of Judgment

An emergency fund is specifically saved for unexpected urgent costs, so it's important not to dip into it for planned purchases or expenses. Remember, if you can foresee an expense, it's not an emergency. Appropriate uses of the fund could be medical emergencies, urgent household repairs, unexpected auto repairs, and income loss.

2.6. The "No-Touch" Rule and Rebuilding Your Fund

It is best to apply a 'no-touch' rule to your emergency fund for things that aren't emergencies. Once used, prioritize refilling the fund as quickly as possible.

Prioritizing saving after depleting your emergency savings might seem like we're asking you to climb a mountain after just descending one. But reestablishing your financial safety net swiftly is key, for you never know when life might throw another curveball your way.

2.7. Final Thoughts

Understanding the basics and utility of an emergency fund is the first step towards financial resilience. Start today, no matter how small. A little can go a long way when planning for your future financial stability.

Remember, an emergency fund is not a static entity - it's a dynamic portion of your financial portfolio that needs attention and reassessment. By establishing and maintaining your emergency fund, you invest in peace of mind and protect yourself and your loved ones from the unexpected financial perils of life. The essence of it isn't merely surviving unforeseen circumstances but thriving in them.

Finally, remember that this process is personalized, based on an individual's circumstances. Customizing your emergency fund to your needs will go a long way in making sure you stay resilient during challenging times. It isn't a hallmark of financial pessimism, but a pillar of financial optimism.

Chapter 3. Why You Need an Emergency Fund: Examining the Necessity

Before we delve deep into the mechanics of building an emergency fund, let's first establish why you need one. It's often easy to live in the present, pay bills, occasionally indulge, and pretty much ignore the thought of something unexpected happening. But life is, by nature, unpredictable.

Financial advisors across the board agree that maintaining an emergency fund is a fundamental aspect of any sound financial plan. But why is that the case?

3.1. The Unpredictability of Life

Life is full of uncertainty. Jobs are lost, cars break down, medical emergencies arise, natural disasters occur - the list of what could go wrong is virtually endless.

An emergency fund is a financial buffer specifically designated to cover these unexpected expenses. By providing a financial safety net, such a fund ensures that these emergencies don't turn into severe crises that push you into debt or financial instability. Simply put, an emergency fund is insurance for your wellbeing and peace of mind.

3.2. Weathering Financial Storms

When an unexpected expense arises, the first instinct is often to turn towards credit cards or loans. While these options may provide immediate relief, in the long run, they add to your liabilities, leading to increased indebtedness.

An emergency fund acts as a bulwark against this debt cycle. If your car suddenly needs a costly repair, your emergency fund helps you meet that expense without having to rely on expensive credit. This buffer allows you to negotiate financial challenges in the short term without jeopardizing your long-term financial health.

3.3. Avoiding Premature Withdrawals from Investment Accounts

Over time, wise investments can significantly contribute towards wealth creation. However, utilizing these funds prematurely in times of crisis can thwart your long-term financial goals.

In addition to losing potential profits, early withdrawals from tax-advantaged accounts like 401ks, IRAs, or certain types of savings plans can lead to high penalties and extra tax payments. With an emergency fund, you can avoid dipping into these accounts and ensure your investments continue to grow undisturbed.

3.4. Coping With Income Loss

Whether it's due to sudden unemployment, illness preventing work, or a global pandemic, the risk of income loss is always looming. In such cases, an emergency fund can provide you with a necessary financial bridge, helping to cover basic living expenses until you're able to return to work or find a new job. Some financial advisors recommend having enough saved to cover 3-6 months of living expenses, though this exact figure can vary depending on your individual circumstances.

3.5. Achieving Financial Independence

Regardless of your financial goals, an emergency fund is a vital step towards achieving financial independence. It gives you the freedom to make choices – to switch jobs, to take calculated risks, or to refuse a bad deal – all because you are not living paycheck to paycheck.

Being ready for unforeseen expenses also boosts your confidence and alleviates stress, leaving you better equipped to make sound financial decisions. This preparedness spills over into other aspects of your financial life, allowing you to invest more, save more, and spend on things you genuinely value.

3.6. How much to Save?

While the importance of an emergency fund isn't in question, the appropriate size of a fund can be a point of debate. Generally, it's wise to have 3-6 months' worth of essential expenses in your emergency fund. The exact amount, however, will depend on a number of factors including your job security, monthly expenses, the size of your family, and whether or not you have dependents.

Ultimately, the objective is to give yourself a financial cushion that allows you to maintain your current lifestyle during an unexpected crisis without incurring debt or prematurely withdrawing from your long-term investments.

The concept of an emergency fund is incredibly simple, but the effect it can have on your financial wellbeing is profound. Whether you're just starting your financial journey or are well along on your path, understanding the necessity of an emergency fund and incorporating it into your financial strategy can play a pivotal role in achieving financial security and resilience. By preparing for the unexpected, you can ensure that when life throws a curveball, it doesn't derail your financial wellbeing, but instead allows you to steer towards an even stronger financial future.

Chapter 4. Starting Your Fund: Steps to Embark

The very beginning of creating an emergency fund starts with determining the amount you aim to save. Depending on your income and expenses, this amount can vary widely from person to person. However, a good rule of thumb to follow is striving to save three to six months' worth of living expenses.

4.1. Calculate Your Living Expenses

To calculate your living expenses, you need to take into account all costs you would need to cover if your income were to suddenly cease. These costs typically include rent/mortgage, utilities, insurance, groceries, transportation, and any ongoing medical bills. Additionally, it's wise to factor in any outstanding debts you have, like student loans or credit cards. Once you've compiled all these costs, multiply them by the number of months you wish to cover. This gives you your target goal for your emergency fund.

Remember this is an estimate. Your actual expenses may vary, particularly in a crisis situation. Thus, it's always better to overestimate rather than underestimate when it comes to setting up your emergency fund.

4.2. Set a Timeline for Your Saving Goal

Knowing how much you need to save doesn't necessarily make it easier to save that amount. Most of us wouldn't be able to reach our saving goal overnight. Therefore, it's important to set a realistic timeline for reaching your goal. Consider your income, expenses, and any other financial obligations when deciding on the timeframe, and set manageable monthly saving goals that fit within your budget.

4.3. Choose the Right Savings Account

When it comes to where you should keep your emergency fund, the ideal place is in a separate savings account. This separation is important to prevent you from dipping into your emergency fund for everyday expenses. Opt for a high-yield savings account, which will earn you more in interest than a traditional savings account. Also, make sure that your chosen account offers quick and easy access to your funds, in case of an emergency.

NOTE Don't stow your emergency funds where they might be hard to access like in investments like stocks or mutual funds. The point of this fund is to be readily available in a crisis.

4.4. Automating Your Savings

Automating your savings transfers can take the decision-making and willpower out of the equation making it more likely for your emergency fund to grow. You could schedule automatic transfers from your checking to your savings account after each payday.

4.5. Balance Your Savings Goals

While it's important to build your emergency fund, it's also crucial to balance this goal with other financial objectives, like retirement savings or paying off high-interest debts. Striking this balance can be a delicate act. It may be worth seeking advice from a financial advisor to help guide you through this process.

4.6. Regularly Review and Adjust Your Plan

As life changes, so do your financial needs. Changing jobs, moving, major life events like marriage or having a child can all affect your financial situation and the amount you should have in your emergency fund. Review your plan regularly and adjust your savings goals as needed.

Remember, the emergency fund is a dynamic tool that should adapt to your evolving life circumstances. Building it is not a one-off task but a consistent, deliberate practice that can provide you a safety net when you need it most. By effectively starting and managing your emergency fund, you are taking control of your financial future and setting yourself up for a safer, more secure tomorrow.

4.7. Building an Emergency Fund Is a Marathon, Not a Sprint

Building an emergency fund is a long-term goal. Remember, it's okay to start small and increase your contributions as you become more financially stable. Keep in mind that the point of an emergency fund isn't simply to amass a certain sum of money but to establish financial security and peace of mind.

This is not a plan that yields instant results. It requires patience and consistency. However, the rewards, i.e., financial resilience in the face of unexpected circumstances, are well worth the effort.

Setting Your Financial Safety Net: How Much is Enough?

In the arduous journey of securing one's financial future, the first stepping stone is often setting up an emergency fund. An emergency fund serves as a buffer against unexpected financial distress, providing you with the peace of mind and the financial stability required during such times.

Identifying the Need for an Emergency Fund

Many people wonder if they really need an emergency fund. After all, why let your money sit idle in a savings account when it could possibly generate higher returns elsewhere, such as in investments? The answer lies in the unpredictability of life. Emergency funds are meant to cover sudden and unexpected expenses – those that aren't part of your regular monthly budget, but can significantly disrupt your financial stability. Examples include job loss, medical emergencies, urgent home or auto repairs, last-minute travel, or natural disasters.

Keeping some money aside for unforeseen expenses ensures financial security without having to resort to high-interest loans or credit card debts. They are your immediate go-to in times of need. However, the first question that often arises is: how much should you ideally be saving for emergencies?

Determining the Appropriate Amount

There's no one-size-fits-all answer as the amount you may need can significantly depend on a variety of factors, including your lifestyle, monthly expenses, family size, and the nature of your job, amongst others.

Financial advisors conventionally suggest having an emergency fund equivalent to three to six months' worth of living expenses. This typically covers essential costs that you absolutely cannot avoid, like:

- Rent or mortgage

- Groceries

- Utilities

- Health insurance premiums

- Car payments

- Medications

- Childcare

However, this is a general guideline and may or may not be suitable, given your personal circumstances.

If you're single with no dependents, your emergency fund needs may be towards the lower end of that scale. If you're the primary breadwinner of a large family with a mortgage, then a six-month cushion might still not be enough.

In assessing your emergency fund needs, consider the following:

1. The stability of your income: If your income fluctuates or isn't guaranteed (as in freelancing or self-employment), you might want to save more.

2. Your health insurance policy: If your coverage isn't extensive, medical emergencies may require more substantial funds.

3. Dependents: The number of individuals depending on your income will influence how much you need to save.

Building Your Emergency Fund: Step by Step

So, how does one go about saving a lump sum that's equivalent to three to six months' worth of their living expenses? Here are some steps to guide you through:

1. **Start Small**: If saving several months' worth of expenses sounds too ambitious, start with a smaller achievable goal. Aim for $500 first. Once you've saved that, gradually raise the bar.

2. **Save Regularly**: Set aside a fixed sum of money every month. Automate this process so that a certain amount of your paycheck directly goes to your emergency fund, even before you have the chance to spend it.

3. **Treat it as a Bill**: You should treat your monthly savings commitment just like any other bill. Just like how you'd be penalized if you forget to pay your bills, assign a penalty to yourself if you fail to deposit into your emergency fund every month.

4. **Extra Income and Windfalls**: When you receive a bonus, tax refund, inheritance, or any kind of windfall, consider adding part of it to your emergency fund.

5. **Limit Access**: If you know the money is easily accessible, you might be tempted to use it for unnecessary things. So, keep it slightly out of reach.

Using Your Emergency Fund Effectively

After setting up the emergency fund, the challenge is to use it wisely. It's important to clarify that this fund is strictly for emergencies and not to be used for planned expenses or wants. It is for situations when you're out of all other financial options.

Once you've saved enough, don't stop there. Inflation and changing circumstances might mean your emergency fund may not meet your needs in future. Review and adjust the amount in your fund annually.

Having an emergency fund gives you peace of mind and creates a financial safety net. It provides a protective layer to your finances, keeping you prepared for life's curveballs. No matter what your financial status is, it's never too late or too soon to start building an emergency fund. Remember, in the world of personal finance, an emergency fund isn't considered an optional luxury; it's a necessity.

Chapter 5. Thrifty Saving Techniques: Economize to Capitalize

Improving financial resilience and building an emergency fund starts with fixing the leaks in one's budget. Skyrocketing savings begins by mastering frugality and learning to economize wherever possible, making every cent count. Now, let's delve into some practical strategies for thrifty saving that you can implement today to secure your tomorrow.

5.1. Getting Started: The Budget Breakdown

The first step toward thrifty saving and a heftier emergency fund is a comprehensive understanding of your income and expenses. A budget is simply a plan detailing where your money will go each month.

Creating a budget isn't rocket science. Here's a step-by-step guide:

5.2. Economizing Essentials: Slash and Save

4. Review, compare, and adjust: Look over your income and expenses, tweak where it's needed, and work on reaching a state where your income comfortably covers all your expenses with some to spare.

After setting your budget, it would be clear which areas can be adjusted for increased savings. Two broad categories where the big savings often lurk are: Housing and Transportation.

2. Transportation: Commuting by public transport, biking, carpooling, or even going for a more fuel-efficient vehicle can save you a significant sum.

Consider small but repetitive expenses too. These add up over time and trimming them could bring substantial savings that can be directed towards your emergency fund.

5.3. Developing Smart Shopping Habits

Mastering the art of spending less on shopping provides a surplus for savings. Here are few techniques:

5.4. Economizing on Entertainment

5. Learn to negotiate: Try to get a discount wherever possible.

The entertainment category can often be a black hole for money! Here's how to economize:

5.5. Making the Most of Your Meals: Economizing on Food

3. Discounted tickets: Look for cheaper tickets for movies, theaters, etc. during specific days or times.

Food expenses take up a large part of our monthly budget. Here's how you can economize:

5.6. Energize and Economize: Lowering Utility Bills

4. Use leftovers: Get creative with the remaining food instead of throwing it away.

Utilities can take a significant chunk of your budget. But there are ways to be efficient:

5.7. Emergency Fund 101: Applying the Savings

4. Water conservation: Less usage equals lower bills.

Every dollar you save by economizing should be directed towards your emergency fund. Once you've cut back, pay off high-interest debts, if any. Then, start stashing away cash in a special savings account earmarked as your emergency fund.

Building an emergency fund is a marathon, not a sprint. Little by little, a little becomes a lot. With time, effort, and patience, you can build an emergency fund that shields you from financial surprises and lets you capitalize on your thriftiness. After all, 'A penny saved is a penny earned'.

In conclusion, thrifty saving techniques aren't about sacrifice, they're about smart choices. Making incremental changes and forming better habits really can get you to your financial goals faster. Take the time to sit down, examine your situation, and see where you can implement these strategies. No matter how small the change, the positive impact on your financial future will be significant.

Chapter 6. Investing in Your Security: Growth Options for Your Fund

Ensuring your financial security means making provisions for unforeseen circumstances, and investing in the growth of your emergency fund is a surefire way towards financial resilience. But how do you grow your fund? What investment options do you have, and how do you take advantage of them? This chapter delves into growing your emergency fund through smart and strategic investment.

6.1. The Basics: Understanding Investments

Before we delve into the specifics of investing your fund, it's crucial to understand what investing entails. In simple terms, investing involves directing your money or assets towards a venture, with the hopes of achieving a financial return over time. With the right strategies, your emergency fund can grow beyond your regular contributions, making you more financially robust and resilient than ever.

6.2. Safe Investment Options

Investments come with risks. However, since we are looking at an emergency fund – a safety net that you need to rely on in times of need, the goal is to minimize risk. Here are a few low-risk investment options for your emergency fund.

- **High-Yield Savings Accounts:** High-yield savings accounts offer a higher interest rate than regular savings accounts, ensuring your money grows while remaining accessible.

- **Money Market Accounts:** Similar to savings accounts, but often come with checking account features as well. They tend to provide higher interest rates than regular savings accounts.

- **Certificates of Deposit (CDs):** These are time-specific investments with a fixed interest rate. Your initial deposit and any accumulated interest are returned after a predetermined period. The disadvantage is the lack of liquidity.

Remember that these options promise modest returns - they're not meant to make you wealthy but rather to ensure that your emergency fund keeps pace with inflation and grows steadily.

6.3. Formulate an Investment Strategy

Planning is key to effective investing. Here's a simple guide to help you formulate your investment strategy:

1. **Determine your Risk Appetiteness:** How much financial risk are you comfortable with? Low-risk investments usually offer lower returns, while high-risk investments potentially offer higher returns (or larger losses).

2. **Set Clear Goals:** What do you want to achieve with your investments? Knowing your financial goals helps you monitor your progress and motivates you to stay on track.

3. **Allocate Your Assets:** This is how you divide your investments among different types. A typical strategy might include a mix of cash, bonds, and shares.

4. **Diversify:** Don't put all your eggs in one basket. The key to minimizing risk and maximizing return is to diversify.

5. **Re-evaluate Regularly:** Maintain a regular check on your investments to adjust your strategy as needed.

6.4. Investing Between Fund Categories

Consider maintaining and growing two types of emergency funds. The first is to cover quick, unexpected expenses and can be held in a liquid form (like a savings account). The second is a long-term safety net that can protect you from significant life disruptions (such as losing a job). The second fund is where you can put your investments to work.

6.5. Pitfalls to Avoid

Every investment journey has its challenges. Here are some pitfalls to avoid:

- **Procrastination:** The earlier you start investing, the more time your money has to grow.

- **Investing Without Understanding:** Make sure you understand your investment well.

- **Ignoring Inflation:** Inflation erodes the value of money over time. Make sure your investment gives returns higher than the inflation rate.

- **Letting Emotions Drive Investment Decisions:** Investing is not about winning; it focuses on long-term financial growth.

6.6. The Final Word

Investing in the growth of your fund does involve some risks, but with careful planning, strategic investment, and regular monitoring, you can effectively grow your emergency fund. It's all about taking calculated risks to ensure your investment earns a return that's greater than the inflation rate while not putting your emergency fund at undue risk. After all, the primary goal of an emergency fund is to provide you with financial safety, and growing it safely enhances its ability to do so. Remember, a robust emergency fund is like having an insurance policy against life's financial pitfalls, so it's indeed an investment in your security. Keep learning, keep investing, and keep growing for a financially secure future!

Chapter 7. Tapping into Your Emergency Fund: When and How?

Before we delve into the details of when and how to use your emergency fund, it's important to reiterate the fact that an emergency fund isn't just designed to weather you through minor hiccups; it is established for major crises such as a job loss, medical emergency, or an unexpected major expense. This fund acts as a financial safety net, and knowing when and how to tap into it is crucial in ensuring financial security.

7.1. Recognizing a Financial Emergency

The first step to effectively utilizing your emergency fund is discerning a true financial emergency from a desire or non-critical event. An emergency warrants the use of your fund when:

1. It's unexpected: The event or expense was not anticipated, such as sudden medical bills or major car repairs.

2. It's urgent: The event or expense requires immediate attention, and delaying it may cause additional financial or emotional distress.

3. It's necessary: The event or expense is non-negotiable, like a utility bill or rent, and not a luxury or optional expense.

Let's examine each of the points above in detail.

Unexpected expenses can include unexpected medical expenses or major car repairs. These are types of immediate requirements that demand monetary resources. However, a new TV or laptop that breaks down, although unexpected, does not necessarily classify as an emergency unless it directly affects your livelihood.

Events or expenses defined as urgent require immediate action. For example, a sudden roof leak during rainy seasons that demands a quick fix, as delaying it will imply further serious damages and costs.

The necessity criterion ensures that the event or expense is absolutely non-negotiable. Say for instance; you are unable to pay this month's rent due to a cut in your wages. Covering such vital expenses from your emergency fund is justified.

Misjudging the purpose of your emergency funds can drastically depreciate its value, leaving you with insufficient protection in the face of an actual emergency. Therefore, it's crucial to evaluate the situation and consider if it meets these criteria before dipping into your savings.

7.2. Unlocking Your Emergency Fund

Having properly identified a genuine emergency, the next step is to decide how to withdraw from your emergency fund. Most experts recommend that your emergency fund be readily accessible, such as in a high-yield savings or money market account, so you can quickly pull funds when necessary.

If you've diversified your emergency fund across multiple accounts for better interest rates or security, consider proportitionally withdrawing from each account to maintain the diversifications over a longer period.

Another factor to consider is the tax implications. Certain type of accounts, like a retirement account, may have financial penalties for early withdrawal. In such cases, consider other sources of assets first.

7.3. Replenishing Your Emergency Fund

After an emergency, as soon as you're back on your feet, your top priority should be to reestablish your emergency fund. The sooner you replace the money, the better prepared you'll be for the next crisis.

Dedicate a portion of your income towards replenishing the fund. You can automate this by setting up a direct deposit from your paycheck into your emergency fund. Over time, this allows your fund to recover without straining your regular budget.

Once your fund is back to a level that can sustain your expenses for at least three to six months, you can then revert back to your regular savings plan.

Exhausting your emergency fund can be psychologically draining as it's a glaring reminder of your vulnerability in emergencies. However, remember that you created this safety net precisely for these types of scenarios. Using it doesn't mean you failed; on the contrary, it indicates the success of your plan.

It's important within this process to avoid unnecessary debt. Be disciplined about rebuilding the emergency fund before budgeting for non-essential expenses.

The process of tapping into your emergency fund might seem daunting. It could be a stark reminder of life's volatility and uncertainties. Despite this, being prepared to recognize an emergency, knowing how to extract the resources wisely, and maintaining a recovery plan is vital in surviving and thriving in a crisis.

Chapter 8. Rebuilding After Use: Ensuring Future Financial Safety

Spending from your emergency fund can invoke mixed feelings: relief as it safeguards you from financial stress, but also apprehension over how to rebuild the depleted resources. This chapter aims to inform you about the strategic process of reaccumulating your safe haven while ensuring future financial safety.

8.1. Developing a Strategic Plan

Rebuilding your emergency fund isn't a task you can effectively accomplish at the snap of your fingers. It requires a strategic, well-crafted plan. Start by determining what you spent from the emergency fund and establishing a timeline to replenish those funds. Prioritizing this repayment should be on top of your list and must compete favorably with other financial objectives.

Establishing a timeline helps in drafting a monthly savings target you should strive towards. It needs to be a balance between speed (the quicker, the better) and realistic capacity (don't strangle your daily necessary expenses). With this strategic plan, repayment becomes systematic and achievable.

8.2. Reworking Your Budget

Rebuilding an emergency fund often translates into redefining your budget. Evaluate areas where you can trim expenses without hampering your quality of life significantly. Reducing dining out, opting for a cheaper cable plan, or putting a stop to the monthly subscription boxes you rarely ever use could be some of the changes you implement.

Moreover, windfall incomes like tax refunds, bonuses, or gifts could be directed towards the emergency fund refill. Though the temptation to splurge is high, remember, it is more beneficial to ensure financial safety.

8.3. Exploring Side Hustles

Consider embracing a side hustle to swell your income sources in times of crises. This can be anything — from freelancing, teaching, to selling handcrafted goods. Not only does it help to bolster your fund quicker but can also act as an additional security net in times of job losses or slashes in primary income.

8.4. Maintaining an Emergency-Only Rule

Once an emergency account is used, it's crucial to remember its purpose was for emergencies only - therefore, it should be rebuilt for emergencies only. Stringently define what you perceive as an 'emergency.' Generally, scenarios like job loss, health emergencies, or major house or car repairs qualify.

It's easy to justify dipping into it for other reasons, like a vacation or a shopping spree. However, maintaining discipline is critical to ensuring a buffer always exists between you and financial ruin.

8.5. Automating the Process

One of the most efficient and effective ways to rebuild is by automating contributions to your emergency fund. Automated savings eliminate the potential to be swayed away by short-term temptations. Decide on an amount that gets auto-debited into your emergency fund every time you receive income.

As your financial situation improves, you may want to increase this amount to expedite the rebuilding process. Remember, automation is the silent but robust guard of your secure financial future.

8.6. Regular Monitoring and Updates

Financial situations are dynamic and need constant re-evaluation. A change in job, addendum to family, or a rise in income can entail altered expenses and thus a changed emergency fund requirement. A monthly or quarterly review to assess your financial comfort zone and gauge if you are on the right track is a small but significant step towards achieving impeccable financial discipline.

An emergency fund is less of an option and more of a necessity in contemporary times, where life is enveloped by unpredictability. Having one and knowing how to refill it effectively post-usage can be the line dividing financial stress from security, bankruptcy from solvency.

This chapter aimed to lead you through the replenishment journey while ensuring future financial safety. Remember, the art of maintaining and managing an emergency fund is one that pays off when the going gets tough. Building, using, and rebuilding this fund are stages of a vital financial cycle in your life, one that safeguards you against the unforeseen and helps you prosper amidst it.

Chapter 9. Beyond the Basics: Advancing Your Financial Resilience

While understanding the foundational principles of emergency fund establishment is the first step towards protecting your financial health, there's more to discover to fully develop your financial resilience.

9.1. Moving Beyond the Safety Net: Investing Wisely

An essential part of advancing beyond the initial safety net of an emergency fund is making wise investment choices. With the right investment, your money will work for you even while you're not working, growing your wealth over time.

Investments are not an impromptu avenue to venture. One needs to have an understanding of financial markets, or have an advisor who does. Additionally, you should also identify your risk tolerance. Can you bear the risk of losing your principal amount or are you more of a low-risk investor?

When it comes to investing, here's a simple strategy you could follow:

1. Start with low-risk investments – Government bonds or CDs (Certificate of Deposits) are great ways to start. Their returns may not be sky-high, but they're safe.

2. Rise through medium-risk investments – Once you're comfortable, consider investing in real estate or in crowdfunded projects.

3. Dabble in high-risk investments – If you have an appetite for risk, this is where stocks, commodities, and options trading come into play. Ensure you have a diversified portfolio to spread the risk.

Never forget: The objective of investing is not to get rich quick, but to build wealth steadily over time.

9.2. Budgeting: Your Financial Blueprint

Think of budgeting as the architectural plan for your financial house. It monitors your income, guards against excessive spending, and ensures there's enough left for saving and investment.

A successful budget does not require complex software or spreadsheets. Here's a simplified version:

1. List your monthly income.

2. Categorize your expenses into fixed (like rent, utility bills) and variable (like groceries, entertainment).

3. Deduct the total expenses from your income to find out your balance. A positive number indicates you're earning more than you spend, while a negative number means you need to cut back on your expenses.

This exercise will make it visibly clear where your money is going and how you can better allocate resources to ensure financial stability and growth.

9.3. Insure and Secure: Protecting Your Assets

As you move up in your financial planning, safeguarding your hard-earned assets is crucial. There are several types of insurance policies designed to protect different facets of your life. It could be home insurance, life insurance, health insurance, or even auto insurance.

Meet a trustworthy financial advisor who can guide you in identifying the best policies as per your needs. Remember, every insurance is an investment towards your mental peace and a backup support for your financial stability.

9.4. Debt Management: Complete Financial Freedom

Without proper debt management, one would find it difficult to truly achieve financial resilience and independence.

Here are steps to tackle debts efficiently:

1. List all your debts – From mortgage to credit card bills, make a comprehensive list of all your debts.

2. Prioritize your debts – Not all debts are created equal. Prioritize your debts as per their interest rates and the consequences of not paying them off.

3. Start with the highest priority debt – Pay off the highest priority debt first while paying the minimum required amount on others. After paying it off, go in for the next one, and so on.

Remember to keep your emergency fund intact during this process. The goal of financial resilience is to navigate through financial emergencies, not to create them.

9.5. Consider Passive Income Sources

Creating additional income streams that require little to no effort (passive income) can help bolster your financial resilience.

Here are some options:

1. Rent out a property – If you own an extra property, rent it out. With reliable tenants, this is a steady income source.

2. Peer-to-peer lending platforms – Lend smaller sums of money across multiple businesses or individuals for gaining interest income.

3. Affiliate marketing – If you have a blog or a website, affiliate marketing can let you earn a commission for every customer you direct to a product or service.

By addressing these themes, you can not only survive in times of financial unpredictability, but also prosper. Cultivate these practices and plant the seeds of financial resilience. It's all about advancing step by step, learning along the journey, and letting your money grow and protect you.

Remember, the road to financial resilience is not a sprint but a marathon. By mastering these principles, you're investing in your financial health, your future security, and your peace of mind. So, keep going, and you'll soon see the results of your financial decisions contribute to a more secure and worry-free future.

Chapter 10. Case Studies: Real-Life Success Stories of Emergency Funds

The power of emergency funds cannot be overstated. They can provide a financial buffer during job loss, cover unexpected bills or expenses, offer a safety net during medical emergencies, or help in navigating unforeseen global crises, such as the recent COVID-19 pandemic. Let's delve deeper into some real-life examples that underline the critical importance of keeping a well-stocked emergency fund.

10.1. First Case: Jane - Overcoming Job Loss

Jane was a 35-year-old marketing executive, earning a handsome salary, with a mortgage on a two-bedroom house and a recent foray into expensive hobbies. Living a seemingly comfortable life, she believed she had no reason to worry about a rainy day fund. That was until she was unexpectedly made redundant from her job.

Without an income and without savings, Jane's lifestyle became untenable almost overnight. She managed to scrape by a few months using her meager savings and stretching her credit cards to the limit, but it was clear that a longer-term solution was needed quickly.

Recognizing the need for an emergency fund, Jane began making radical changes in her life. She downgraded her home, cut unnecessary expenses, and funneled every extra penny into her emergency fund.

Eventually, after several difficult months, Jane bounced back. She found a new job, but her emergency fund-building habits were here to stay. She continued living frugally, putting a portion of her income into her emergency fund. Today, Jane has a six-month worth of living expenses in her emergency fund and feels secure about her finances.

10.1.1. Lessons from Jane's Story

Jane's experience highlights some key lessons we can learn:

1. Cut unnecessary expenses: Jane quickly learned the difference between necessities and luxuries, giving up her expensive hobbies and moving to a smaller house to save money.

2. Prioritize the fund: Despite finding a new job, Jane continued saving for her fund, realizing the importance of a safety net.

10.2. Second Case: John and Marcy - Planned for Global Pandemic

John and Marcy, a couple with two young children, epitomize financial prudence. Even with a stable dual income, they've always recognized the importance of an emergency fund. They ensured that they had at least 12 months' worth of living expenses saved up at any time.

When the COVID-19 situation intensified, both John and Marcy found themselves on unpaid leave. Bank account bled dry by bills and daily expenses, they would've been in a dire situation had it not been for their foresight to build an emergency fund.

Their fund not only ensured they could maintain a semblance of normalcy in their kids' lives in the pandemic but also allowed them to focus on securing alternative sources of income.

10.2.1. Lessons from John and Marcy's Story

The key teachings from John and Marcy's experience include:

1. Maintain a substantial fund: A bare minimum emergency fund should cover 3-6 months' worth of expenses, but John and Marcy always aimed for a year. This foresight proved to be a lifesaver during the pandemic.

2. Plan for the unthinkable: Emergencies can come in any form - from personal crises like job loss or illness to global situations like pandemics. It's crucial to be prepared for all possible scenarios.

10.3. Final Thoughts

In conclusion, emergency funds are crucial life rafts that can keep everyone afloat during financial storms. Starting early, saving consistently, distinguishing necessities from luxuries, and preparing for the unthinkable can equip individuals with financial resilience during adverse circumstances. Through the cautionary tales of Jane and the emergency preparedness of John and Marcy, we hope you've realized the importance of building and maintaining a robust emergency fund.